FROZEN IN FEAR

A story of childhood anxiety

By Carol Young
Illustrated by Mary Mamontova

"Frozen in Fear" is a child friendly story that takes a look at childhood anxiety.

The book is my personal journey living with anxiety and how I learned to navigate through these difficult feelings.

Constance is "little Carol."
She is overwhelmed with anxiety yet refuses to be controlled by these emotions.

If you struggle, be bold. Be brave. Find help. Don't give up.

You can do this!

Carol Young

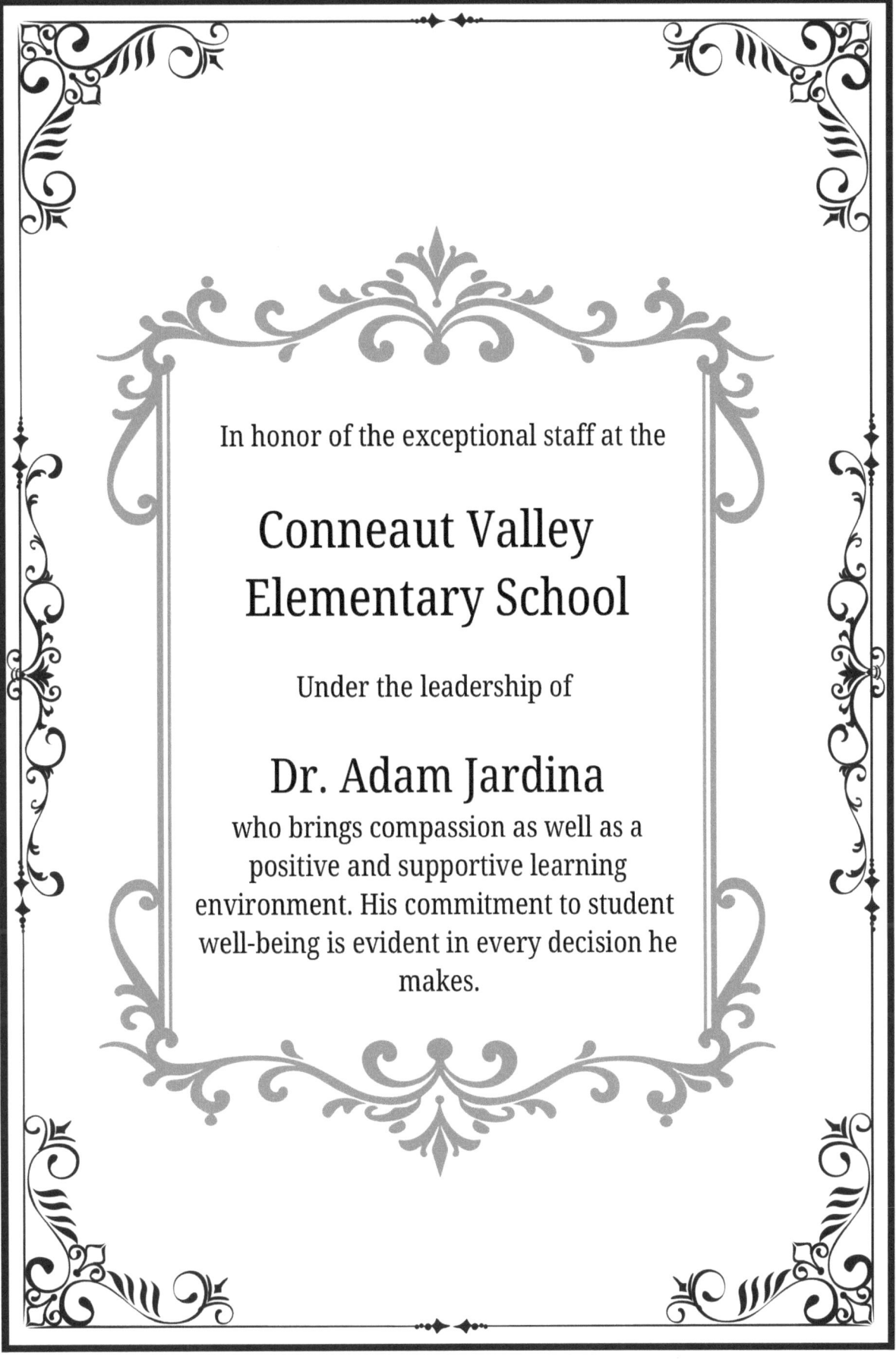

I'm two people all in one,
not twins, but just one daughter.
Some days liquid, some days ice.
An ever changing water.

All people get afraid, I know.
But I'm often plagued with fear.
I've learned to hide my feelings.
I simply disappear.

I'll explain just how it works.
It doesn't make much sense.
I could be playing, having fun,
but then I switch to tense.

It's just the way I am, you see.
I'm happy, then I'm scared.
A liquid pool of feelings streams
from peaceful to impaired.

I might freeze at anytime.
It's really quite a sight.
One simple harmless thought
can trigger overwhelming fright.

There are clues one might see.
My face turns red and hot.
It happens when I'm scared.
I freeze ... my face does not.

You'd think someone would notice
when the freezing part appears.
But I'm an expert at disguise.
I mask all of my fears.

'Cause icebergs do deceive you.
You think you see it all.
But when you look beneath them,
you'll see a giant wall.

Quiet

Sad   Worried

Anxious   Angry

Scared

Not good enough

You say, it's not a big deal.
I tend to disagree.
Freezing stops me in my tracks.
I'm stuck and can't get free.

It begins with something that triggers scary thoughts. Scary thoughts make me freeze. The result? I'm distraught.

Feelings go up and down
like a roller coaster ride.
My tummy's doing flip flops.
Please stop. I'm petrified.

One day a girl asked me to find fun things to do. I said "I can't. I'm different. I get scared. Not like you."

One day a boy asked me
to go outside and walk.
I said "I can't, I'm different.
I'm quiet and can't talk."

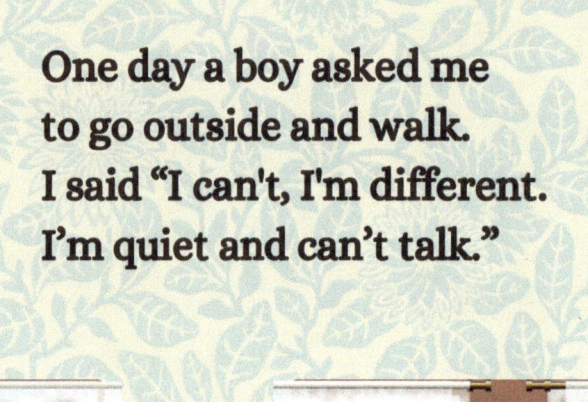

"Constance, please understand
we all believe in you.
Take a chance and try new things.
Your way is Ok too."

"You are talented and bright.
You're the best artist here.
Yes, you are different.
You are special. That is clear."

"When you feel the storm approach
I'll teach you what to do.
Breathe, ground and visualize.
You'll know the tools to use."

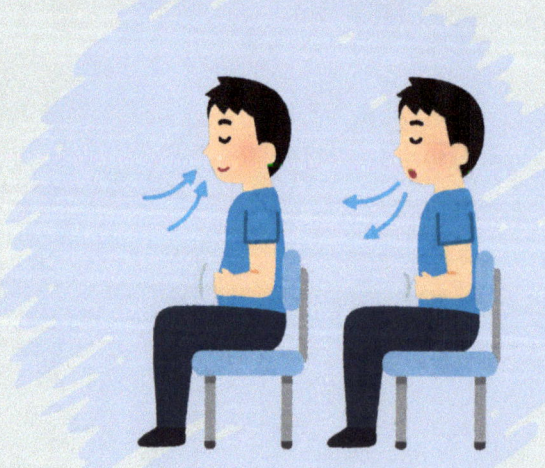

"When those anxious thoughts intrude and make you freeze and cold, stop.
Change your worried mind.
Be positive and bold."

"The bad thoughts have a mission.
They make you feel unwell.
Don't let them win. Fight back.
There are ways to break their spell."

"Simple things like humming
and laughing change your mind.
Change your thoughts to good ones.
The goodness is divine."

"Thawing can be easy.
Thaw to music and to dance.
Thaw when drawing pictures.
Read a book. Take a chance."

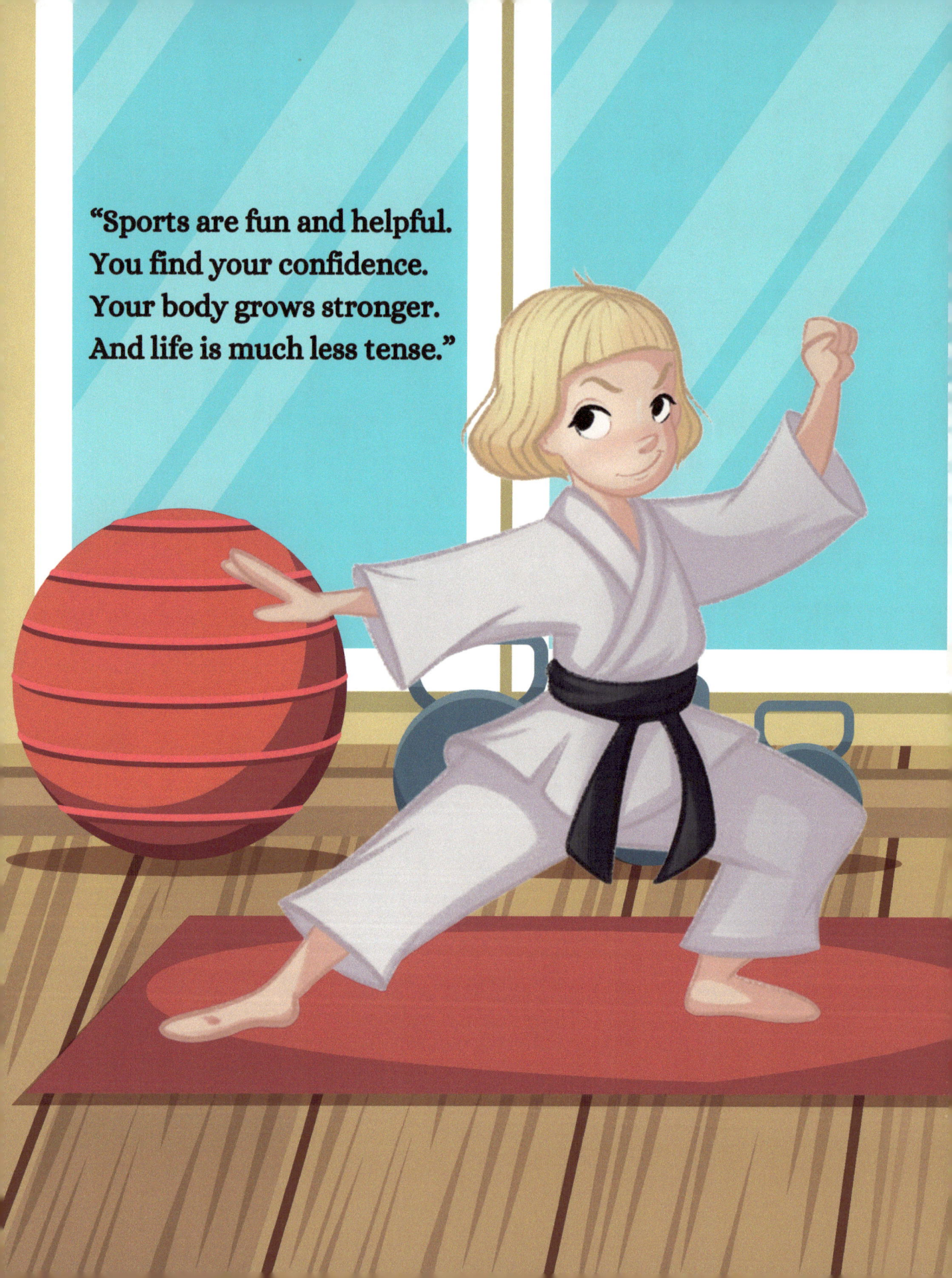

"Sports are fun and helpful.
You find your confidence.
Your body grows stronger.
And life is much less tense."

"Let's say you're afraid
to meet new friends at school.
You think they'll say 'no'
and you're boring, not cool."

"That thought can be scary.
'What if? What if that's true?'
Visualize ways to act
so you'll know just what to do."

"When you go to a party
your ice begins to form.
Friends laugh, eat, sing and dance
while you try to calm your storm."

"No problem! You can do this.
You can turn this thing around
by taking soothing breaths.
You relax and rebound."

"School lunch can be a problem.
You do not want your food.
The noise is overwhelming.
You want some solitude."

"There's no need to worry
cause you need a calmer space.
Your teacher helps you move
to a better, peaceful place."

Is this change possible?
Anxiety is strong.
I'm afraid I can't defrost.
It's hard or am I wrong?

But then I thought of something new
I'd been too cold to see.
I have a choice to ponder.
I can freeze or choose "be free."

At school I don't like recess.
I freeze and can't play games.
I lose my voice and cannot talk.
Anxiety's to blame.

Do I panic? Not a chance!
I play "I Spy." It grounds me.
Finding things I hear and see,
returns me to reality.

Fear is very powerful.
Enough to paralyze.
But deep inside I'm stronger.
It's time to seize the prize.

It's time to take a chance.
It's time to take control.
It may not be so easy.
But thawing is my goal.

Despite my frozen feelings,
I can conquer any task.
I am a superhero.
I do not need to mask.

So when the blizzards come
and threats of frost appear
I know my true identity.
I'm a conqueror of fear!

"Constance, mom is proud of you.
You are stronger every day.
Melting 'cold feet' step by step.
Brave and bold in every way."

I said this tale was scary
because freezing storms are true.
But fear no longer rules me.
I know just what to do.

"You are braver than you believe,
stronger than you seem,
and smarter than you think."

A. A. Milne

TRY THESE THINGS TO CALM YOURSELF

Breathe deeply
Use all 5 senses
Visualize ways to act
Exercise
Have positive thoughts
Listen to happy music
Dance
Sing a song
Find a hobby
Try new things
Laugh
Take chances
Participate in a sport
Enjoy nature
Try yoga

CAROL'S FAVORITE: ROCK IN A ROCKING CHAIR

WAYS TO HELP

Cognitive behavioral therapy (CBT) can help you make sense of overwhelming problems by breaking them down into smaller parts.

In CBT, problems are broken down into 4 main areas:
- situations
- thoughts
- emotions-feelings
- actions

Your thoughts about a certain situation can often affect how you feel both physically and emotionally, as well as how you act in response.

Ask your doctor sbout eye movement desensitization and reprocessing (EMDR) therapy.

It is ok to FEEL...

HAPPY	ANGRY	SAD	EXCITED
JEALOUS	SURPRISED	BORED	EMBARRASSED
CONFUSED	TIRED	SHY	SILLY
DISAPPOINTED	WORRIED	SCARED	FRUSTRATED

Grounding Techniques for the Senses

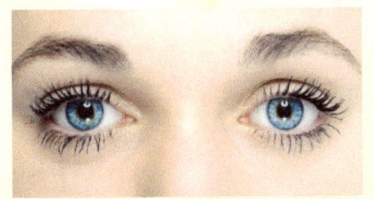
5 THINGS YOU SEE

4 THINGS YOU TOUCH

3 THINGS YOU HEAR

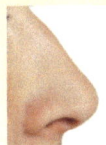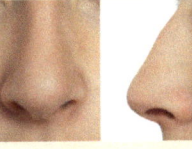
2 THINGS YOU SMELL

1 THING YOU TASTE

Deep Breathing

To help children with anxiety by using deep breathing, teach them "belly breathing" techniques, where they focus on inhaling deeply through their noses, making their bellies expand, and then slowly exhaling through their mouths, contracting their bellies.

Masking

Emotional masking is when someone hides their true feelings and emotions. It can be a coping mechanism to protect oneself from judgment or to fit in with social expectations.

2025

www.ingramcontent.com/pod-product-compliance
Lightning Source LLC
Chambersburg PA
CBHW041536040426

42446CB00002B/106